SEE **BUMBLEBEE** IN AMAZING LIFESIZE!

DRIVE **SIDESWIPE** THROUGH YOUR ROOM IN HIS ALT MODE!

BATTLE YOUR FAVOURITE **AUTOBOTS** AND **DECEPTICONS** AGAINST EACH OTHER!

This is a Carlton Book

HASBRO and its logo, TRANSFORMERS, TRANSFORMERS
ROBOTS IN DISGUISE, the logo and all related characters
are trademarks of Hasbro and are used with permission.

Published in 2016 by Carlton Books Limited. An imprint of the Carlton
Publishing Group, 20 Mortimer Street, London, W1T 3JW.

A catalogue record for this book is available from the British Library.

ISBN 978-1-78312-242-4

Printed in Dongguan, China

Author: Caroline Rowlands
Executive Editor: Alexandra Koken
Design: Darren Jordan
Design Manager: Emily Clarke
Design Director: Russell Porter
Production: Charlotte Larcombe

Need some help? Check out the instructions
at the back of this book and our useful website
for tips and problem-solving advice:
www.icarlton.co.uk/help

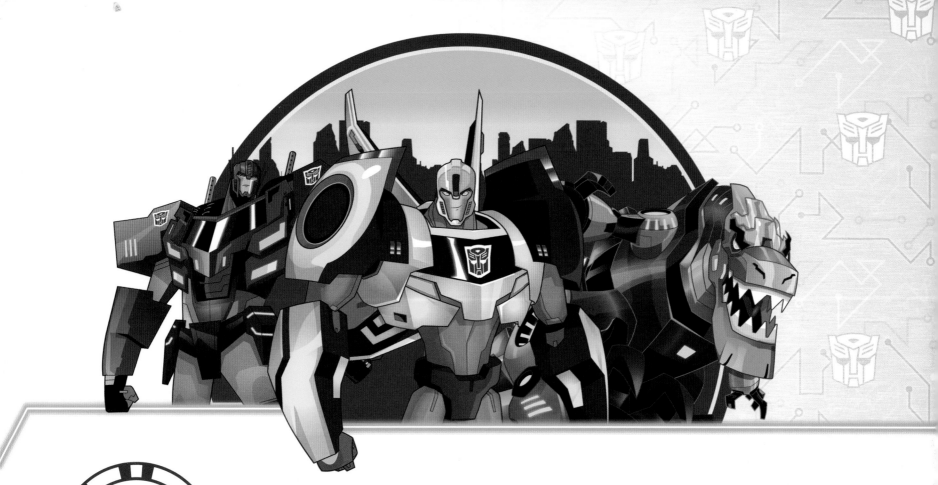

TRANSFORMERS™
ROBOTS IN DISGUISE
WHERE CROWN CITY COMES TO LIFE

CARLTON KIDS

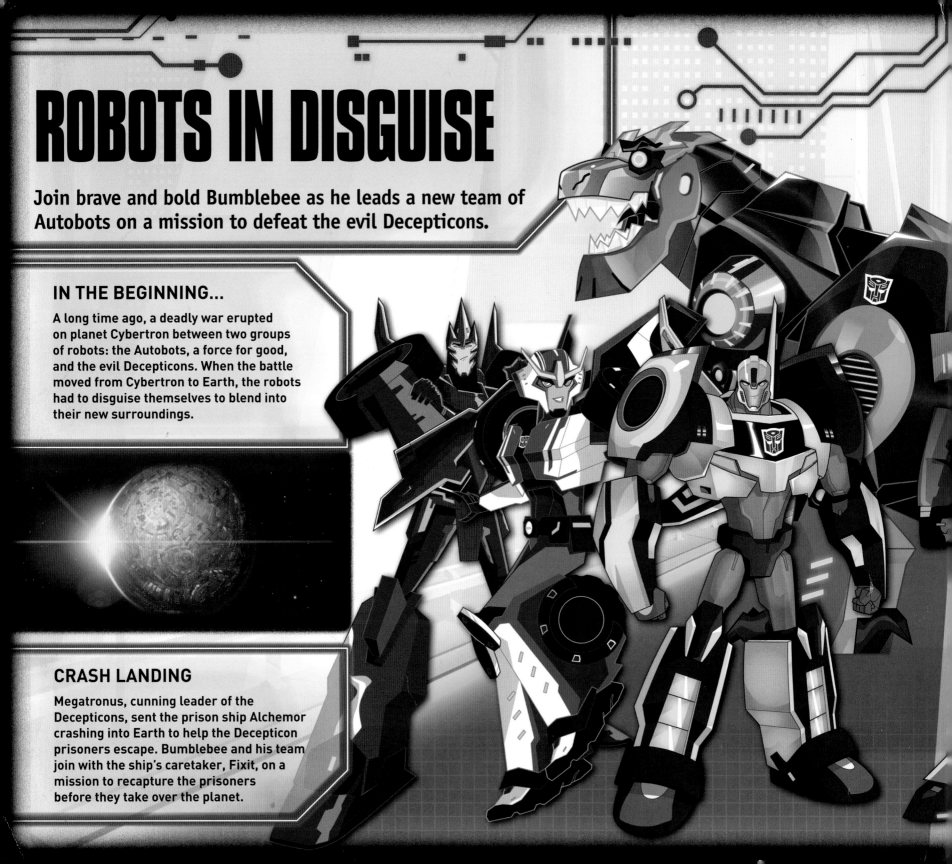

ROBOTS IN DISGUISE

Join brave and bold Bumblebee as he leads a new team of Autobots on a mission to defeat the evil Decepticons.

IN THE BEGINNING...

A long time ago, a deadly war erupted on planet Cybertron between two groups of robots: the Autobots, a force for good, and the evil Decepticons. When the battle moved from Cybertron to Earth, the robots had to disguise themselves to blend into their new surroundings.

CRASH LANDING

Megatronus, cunning leader of the Decepticons, sent the prison ship Alchemor crashing into Earth to help the Decepticon prisoners escape. Bumblebee and his team join with the ship's caretaker, Fixit, on a mission to recapture the prisoners before they take over the planet.

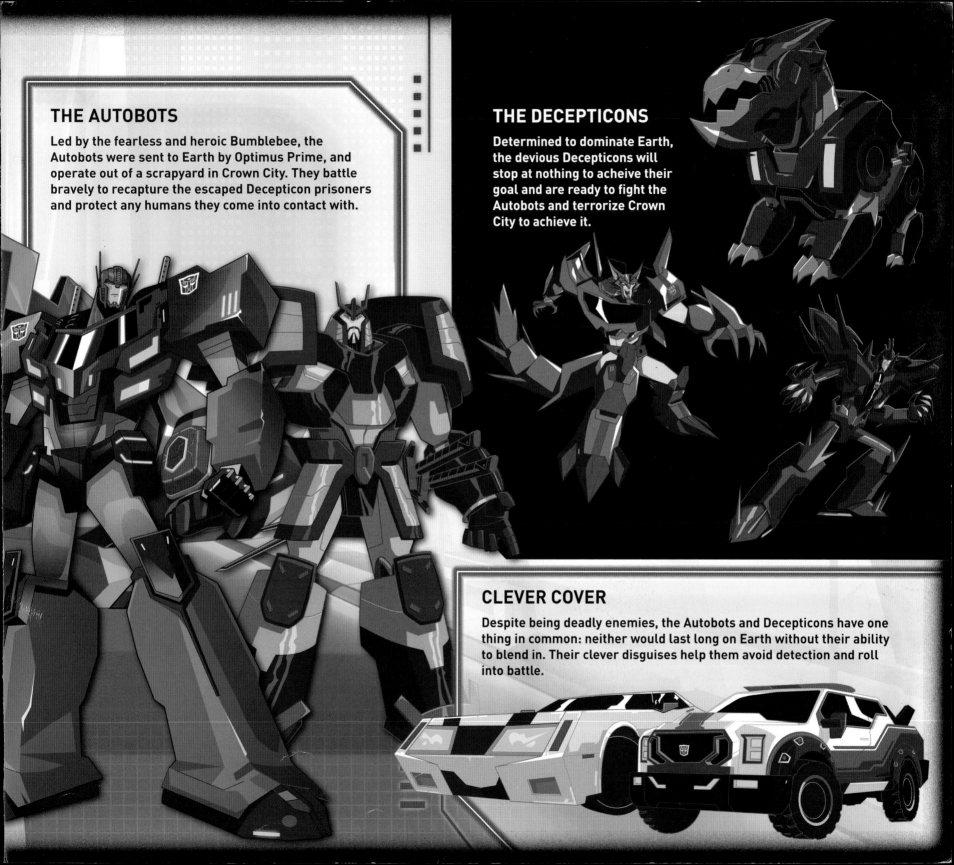

THE AUTOBOTS

Led by the fearless and heroic Bumblebee, the Autobots were sent to Earth by Optimus Prime, and operate out of a scrapyard in Crown City. They battle bravely to recapture the escaped Decepticon prisoners and protect any humans they come into contact with.

THE DECEPTICONS

Determined to dominate Earth, the devious Decepticons will stop at nothing to acheive their goal and are ready to fight the Autobots and terrorize Crown City to achieve it.

CLEVER COVER

Despite being deadly enemies, the Autobots and Decepticons have one thing in common: neither would last long on Earth without their ability to blend in. Their clever disguises help them avoid detection and roll into battle.

OPTIMUS PRIME

Lost in an in-between realm, the strong and powerful former leader of the Autobots Optimus Prime appears to Bumblebee as a vision to guide him on his mission.

HEROIC HELPER

While Optimus Prime isn't always on Earth to help Team Bee, his all-powerful presence is never far away. Bumblebee can always rely on his loyal mentor to guide him with wise words and motivate him to be a tough leader.

TOUGH TRUCK

After training in the Realm of Primes in preparation for a new mission, Optimus Prime eventually comes to Earth. He uses his alt mode of a powerful truck to disguise himself from humans and enemy bots.

AFFILIATION: Autobot
ROLE: Mentor
ALT MODE: Truck
MOST LIKELY TO: Give good advice

BRAVE BATTLES

Admired by both his friends and foes, Optimus Prime's heroic and legendary status has not come easily. He has led the Autobots through many dangerous challenges, helping them escape a doomed Cybertron and battling and defeating the evil Megatronus.

SUPREME STRENGTH

While teaching Bumblebee to capture the escaped Decepticon prisoners, Optimus Prime is being trained by the other original Primes to become something no other Prime has ever achieved: a Supreme.

MAKE OPTIMUS PRIME COME ALIVE!

Activate Optimus Prime with your mobile device to see him lifesize and transform from bot to truck and back!

BUMBLEBEE

As the new leader of the Autobots, Bumblebee's first mission is a tough one – but this loyal and adventurous robot is up for the challenge!

GO BUMBLEBEE!

At first Bumblebee doubts he can live up to his mentor Optimus Prime's high expectations and become a good leader. His brave spirit helps him rise to the challenge but he gets frustrated by his team... and his inability to think of a good catchphrase!

AFFILIATION: Autobot
ROLE: Leader
ALT MODE: Sports car
MOST LIKELY TO: Do the right thing
CAPTURE TECHNIQUE: Plasma cannons

FAST FIGHTER

Smaller than the average robot, Bumblebee makes up for his size with his speed and boundless energy. His alt mode as a sports car helps him rev up, roll out and race towards danger.

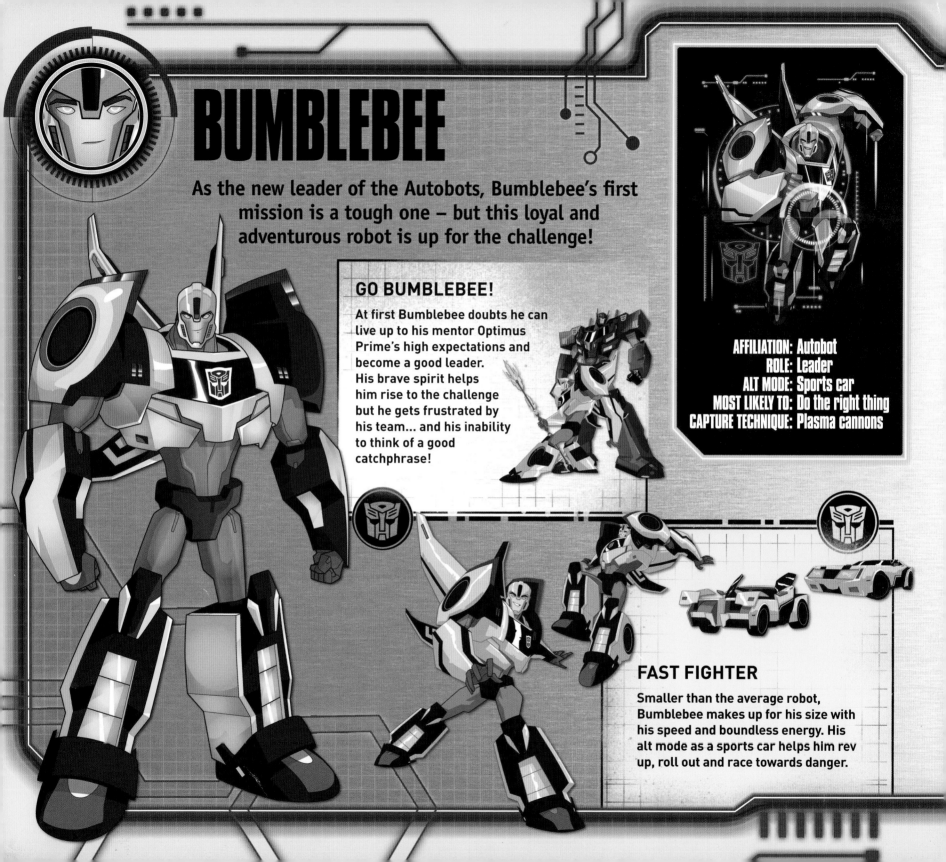

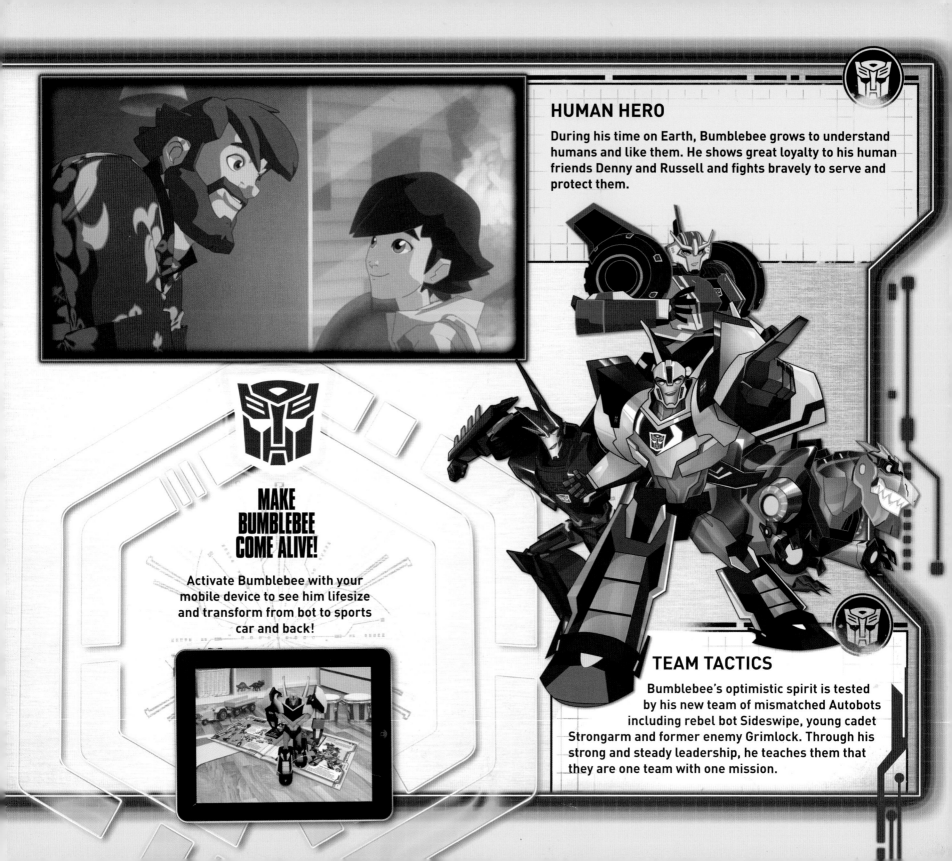

HUMAN HERO

During his time on Earth, Bumblebee grows to understand humans and like them. He shows great loyalty to his human friends Denny and Russell and fights bravely to serve and protect them.

MAKE BUMBLEBEE COME ALIVE!

Activate Bumblebee with your mobile device to see him lifesize and transform from bot to sports car and back!

TEAM TACTICS

Bumblebee's optimistic spirit is tested by his new team of mismatched Autobots including rebel bot Sideswipe, young cadet Strongarm and former enemy Grimlock. Through his strong and steady leadership, he teaches them that they are one team with one mission.

STRONGARM

This tough cadet has dedicated her career to enforcing the law and when she gets her dream job in Bumblebee's team, she's eager to prove she's tough stuff!

AFFILIATION: Autobot
ROLE: Cadet
ALT MODE: Modified police SUV
MOST LIKELY TO: Follow the rule book
CAPTURE TECHNIQUE: Energy axe

OUT FOR ACTION

Living up to her law-enforcing reputation, Strongarm disguises herself as a police vehicle, zooming to the rescue when danger threatens Crown City. Outraged by any criminal behaviour, her strong sense of justice drives her to defeat the Decepticons.

ROBOT RECRUIT

Young cadet Strongarm grew up hearing about the amazing adventures of her heroes Optimus Prime and Bumblebee. She can't believe she is finally a part of her idols' team and is determined to do everything in her power not to let Bumblebee down.

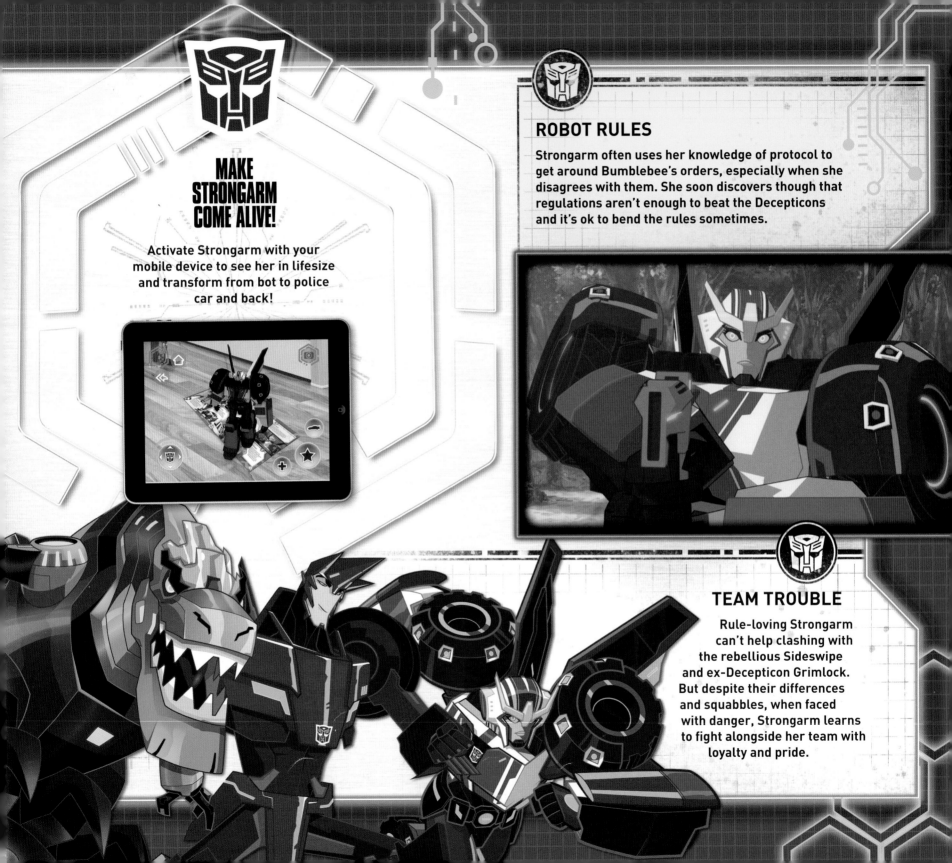

MAKE STRONGARM COME ALIVE!

Activate Strongarm with your mobile device to see her in lifesize and transform from bot to police car and back!

ROBOT RULES

Strongarm often uses her knowledge of protocol to get around Bumblebee's orders, especially when she disagrees with them. She soon discovers though that regulations aren't enough to beat the Decepticons and it's ok to bend the rules sometimes.

TEAM TROUBLE

Rule-loving Strongarm can't help clashing with the rebellious Sideswipe and ex-Decepticon Grimlock. But despite their differences and squabbles, when faced with danger, Strongarm learns to fight alongside her team with loyalty and pride.

SIDESWIPE

Street-smart rebel bot Sideswipe thinks fast and moves even faster. Used to operating alone, he looks out for himself but is always up for action and adventure.

AFFILIATION: Autobot
ROLE: Rebel
ALT MODE: Racing car
MOST LIKELY TO: Break the rules
CAPTURE TECHNIQUE: Cybertanium swords

RACING ROBOT

Back on Cybertron, Sideswipe was a successful racer until he was arrested for speeding by Strongarm. Cuffed and unable to escape, he helped Strongarm and Bumblebee gain access to the space bridge and ended up following them to Earth.

BATTLE BUDDIES

Humans Denny and Russell Clay live in a scrapyard near the Alchemor crash site and help the Autobots on their mission. Russell looks up to Sideswipe and often helps him devise plans to capture the Decepticons.

SOLO FIGHTER

Used to acting alone, Sideswipe often puts missions at risk by only thinking of himself. He slowly learns to trust his Autobot allies and work together as a team, ready to roll to the rescue when duty calls.

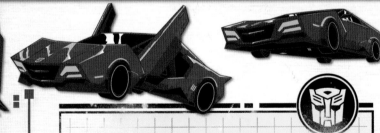

COOL MOVES

Sideswipe's alt mode is a speedy racing car, as fast and competitive as his quick mind. This confident bot enjoys the thrill of the chase but is calm under pressure. He loves playing the part of the cool hero and rolling in to save the day.

MAKE SIDESWIPE COME ALIVE!

Activate Sideswipe with your mobile device to see him lifesize and transform from bot to racing car and back!

FIXIT

This Mini-Con is a human-sized robot that repairs or enhances other Transformers. Fixit may be small but he plays a vital role in Bumblebee's team.

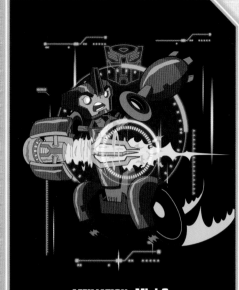

AFFILIATION: Mini-Con
ROLE: Tech geek
ALT MODE: Tools
MOST LIKELY TO: Fix it
CAPTURE TECHNIQUE: Uses technology

TRUSTY TRACKER

Fixit was caretaker of the Alchemor and looked after its prisoners before the crash. What he lacks in battle experience he makes up for in his knowledge of the Decepticon prisoners, helping track and recapture them when they threaten Crown City.

HANDY HELPER

With wheels instead of feet, this nifty little bot scoots around and can change into different tools. Fixit can repair all kinds of things, including the Autobots and the weapons they need for their missions.

MOTOR MOUTH

After being left alone on the Alchemor for so long, Fixit has a few loose wires causing him to muddle up his words and say the wrong thing. Luckily he is still a technical whizz and his skills are vital to Team Bee to help track down the Decepticons.

MAKE FIXIT COME ALIVE!

Activate Fixit with your mobile device and drive him around your room!

TEAM WORK

The Autobots set up their mission headquarters in Denny Clay's scrapyard. It's from here Fixit helps recapture the escaped prisoners and handles all the tech and gadgets. At first Fixit clashes with Denny and tells him Cybertronian technology is too complicated for humans to understand. When Russell turns up with a Decepticon Hunter that's about to explode, Fixit has to work with Denny to fix it and realizes they make a great team.

GRIMLOCK

The warrior Dinobot Grimlock likes to fight hard and play even harder. He never misses out on any fighting fun and loves to beat the bad guys.

AFFILIATION: Dinobot
ROLE: Tough fighter
ALT MODE: Tyrannosaurus rex
MOST LIKELY TO: Smash things
CAPTURE TECHNIQUE: Laser-fire breath

READY TO RRRRRUMBLE!

Grimlock was held prisoner on Alchemor for causing damage on Cybertron. Managing to break free when the ship crashed into Earth, he helps Bumblebee fight and defeat Underbite, earning himself a place on Team Bee.

DINO TERROR

Grimlock's alt mode is a mechanical Tyrannosaurus rex, not the best disguise on planet Earth! Bumblebee realizes what a powerful and strong ally this Dinobot is though, and that Grimlock has huge strength and an even bigger heart.

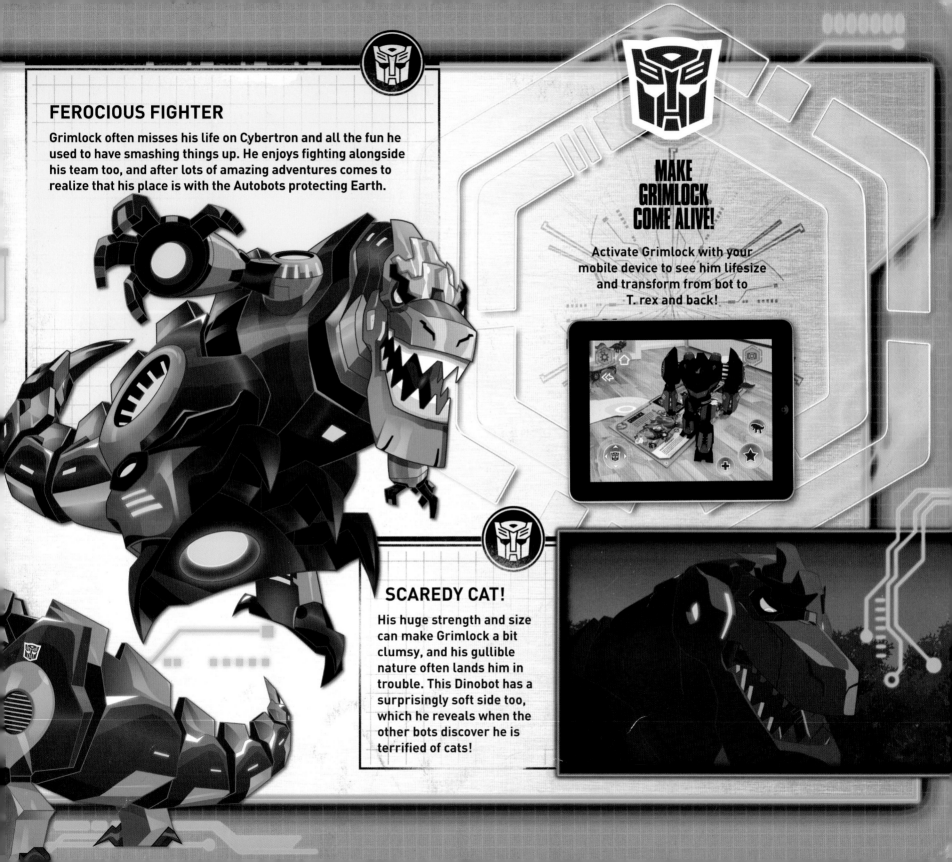

FEROCIOUS FIGHTER

Grimlock often misses his life on Cybertron and all the fun he used to have smashing things up. He enjoys fighting alongside his team too, and after lots of amazing adventures comes to realize that his place is with the Autobots protecting Earth.

MAKE GRIMLOCK COME ALIVE!

Activate Grimlock with your mobile device to see him lifesize and transform from bot to T. rex and back!

SCAREDY CAT!

His huge strength and size can make Grimlock a bit clumsy, and his gullible nature often lands him in trouble. This Dinobot has a surprisingly soft side too, which he reveals when the other bots discover he is terrified of cats!

STEELJAW

The powerful and cunning Steeljaw emerges as the leader of the Decepticons and will stop at nothing to conquer Earth.

LETHAL LEADER

Steeljaw has no respect for the Autobots and their laws. Determined to make Earth the Decepticons' new home, he uses his cunning and strength to lead the Decepticons into battle to defeat Team Bee and take over the planet.

AFFILIATION: Decepticon
ROLE: Mastermind leader
ALT MODE: Off-road vehicle
MOST LIKELY TO: Destroy Earth
CAPTURE TECHNIQUE: Deadly claw

MAKE STEELJAW COME ALIVE!

Activate Steeljaw with your mobile device to see him lifesize and transform from bot to off-road vehicle.

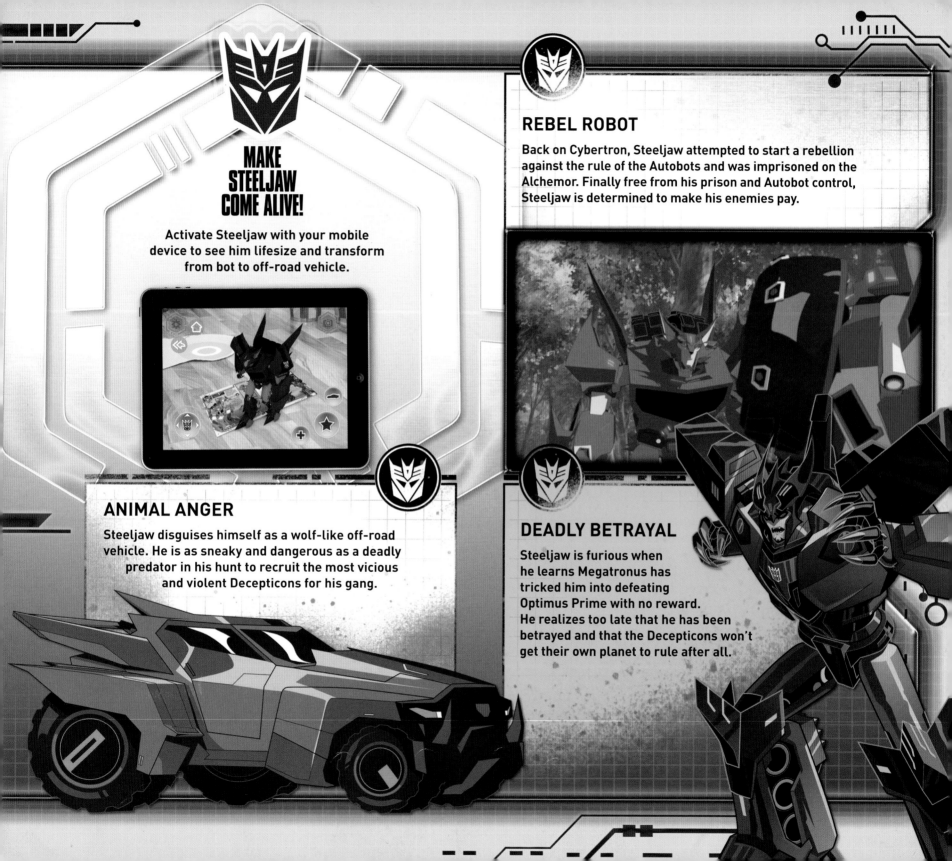

ANIMAL ANGER

Steeljaw disguises himself as a wolf-like off-road vehicle. He is as sneaky and dangerous as a deadly predator in his hunt to recruit the most vicious and violent Decepticons for his gang.

REBEL ROBOT

Back on Cybertron, Steeljaw attempted to start a rebellion against the rule of the Autobots and was imprisoned on the Alchemor. Finally free from his prison and Autobot control, Steeljaw is determined to make his enemies pay.

DEADLY BETRAYAL

Steeljaw is furious when he learns Megatronus has tricked him into defeating Optimus Prime with no reward. He realizes too late that he has been betrayed and that the Decepticons won't get their own planet to rule after all.

UNDERBITE

The metal-munching Underbite is a fierce and ferocious fighter. He is quickly recruited to be part of Steeljaw's deadly Decepticon gang.

AFFILIATION: Decepticon
ROLE: Fierce fighter
ALT MODE: Tank
MOST LIKELY TO: Munch metal
CAPTURE TECHNIQUE: Gnashing jaws

BIG BITE

Underbite was imprisoned on the Alchemor after he ate an entire Cybertronian city, a deadly feat he is very proud of. He loves to talk about his huge stomach and bulging muscles and constantly boasts about how amazing he is.

TOUGH TANK

This deadly Decepticon disguises himself as a futuristic Cybertronian tank-like vehicle. His first mission after escaping the Alchemor is to find some food. His greed often gets him into trouble and distracts him from protecting himself and his gang.

AWESOME APPETITE

The more metal he munches the bigger Underbite becomes, growing stronger with every bite. He admires his powerful muscles so much he names his strong arms Thundercruncher and Boltsmasher. Ouch!

FIGHTING FUEL

Underbite's strength is hard to beat but he needs a steady supply of metal to fuel his power. Without food his energy drains quickly and he becomes weak and easily defeated.

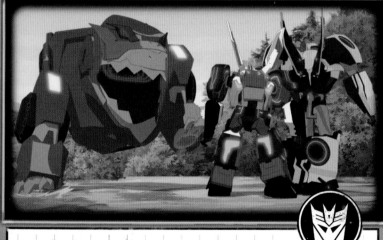

GET INTO BATTLE MODE!

Grab a friend and each activate the AR from this page, then select your Autobot and Deception and battle each other!

THUNDERHOOF

Scheming and clever Thunderhoof joins forces with Steeljaw and the other Decepticons to battle the Autobots, so he can return to his home on Cybertron.

CRIMINAL MASTERMIND

Back on Cybertron, Thunderhoof ran a huge criminal empire with lots of tough bots working for him. Imprisoned on the Alchemor for his dodgy dealings, cunning Thunderhoof seizes his chance and escapes after the crash, determined to get home.

AFFILIATION: Decepticon
ROLE: Former boss
ALT MODE: Tractor
MOST LIKELY TO: Break the law
CAPTURE TECHNIQUE: Powerful hoof stomp

BRIDGE BUILDER

Thunderhoof disguises himself as a tractor on Earth and persuades some humans to help him build a space bridge to get back to Cybertron. His plans go wrong when he can't find a generator to power it, and he ends up stranded on Earth.

SOLID STOMP

When anything or anyone threatens Thunderhoof, he pounds his strong and powerful hoof into the ground sending out a seismic wave. You mess with the boss, you get the hoof!

GANGING UP

Thunderhoof plans to start a new criminal empire on Earth but then meets Steeljaw, who convinces him to join his Decepticon gang. Believing this will help him get home Thunderhoof agrees, even though he hates the fact he's no longer the boss!

SMART STRENGTH

The Autobots never underestimate their dangerous opponent Thunderhoof. He's clever enough to convince others to do his dirty work and tough enough to back up his orders with violence.

DANGEROUS DECEPTICONS

It's not only escaped prisoners that Bumblebee and his team have to battle – there are other deadly Decepticons on Earth too, all seeking to destroy the Autobots.

DANGEROUS HUNTER

A money-grabbing bounty hunter, Fracture will do anything to hunt and capture his victim. No trick is too underhand for this cunning Decepticon who arrives on Earth to capture Bumblebee.

DEADLY STRIKE

After the Alchemor crash, the Sharkticon Hammerstrike dives into Earth's waterways, escaping capture and dry land. Once Cybertron's deadliest pirate, this slippery predator is just as fearsome on Earth, attacking his victims and the Autobots with his razor teeth.

DECEPTICON GANG

When Fracture's ship gets hijacked by the Autobots, he ends up stranded on Earth and decides to join Steeljaw's gang. He helps Underbite and Thunderhoof capture Strongarm and attempts to kidnap Fixit but the Autobots fight back and defeat him.

MINI MENACE

The Mini-Con Airazor joins Fracture on his bounty-hunting mission to capture Bumblebee. What he lacks in brains he makes up for in sneakiness. This tiny terror delights in danger and is a real menace to the Autobots.

DEADLY DIVEBOMB

Airazor's partner in crime is the tiny troublemaker Divebomb. He uses his sharp claws to carve up his enemies and is a master at destroying a target's security and support systems.

TOUGH AS NAILS

The Buffaloid Terrashock is as strong as they come... but doesn't have the brains to match his power. Fiercely loyal, he is searching for his former boss Contrail on Earth, and stops at nothing to find him.

AUTOBOT ALLIES

During their mission on Earth, Bumblebee and his team meet other brave bots and humans, all willing and eager to help defeat the evil Decepticons.

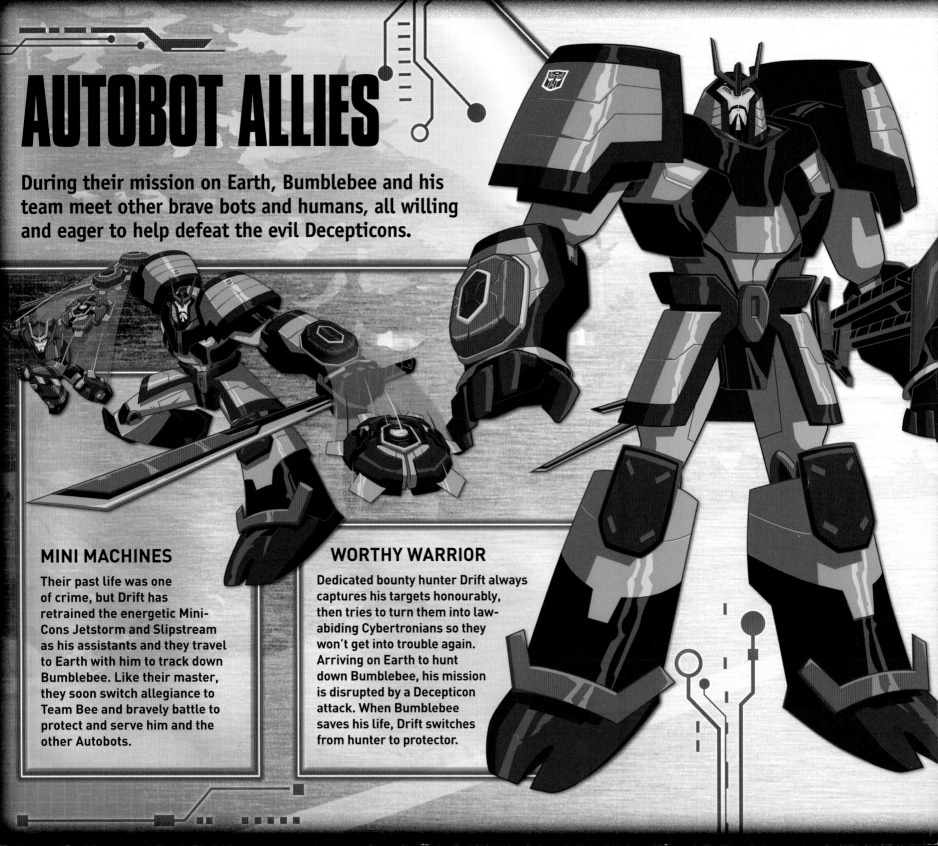

MINI MACHINES

Their past life was one of crime, but Drift has retrained the energetic Mini-Cons Jetstorm and Slipstream as his assistants and they travel to Earth with him to track down Bumblebee. Like their master, they soon switch allegiance to Team Bee and bravely battle to protect and serve him and the other Autobots.

WORTHY WARRIOR

Dedicated bounty hunter Drift always captures his targets honourably, then tries to turn them into law-abiding Cybertronians so they won't get into trouble again. Arriving on Earth to hunt down Bumblebee, his mission is disrupted by a Decepticon attack. When Bumblebee saves his life, Drift switches from hunter to protector.

BATTLE BLASTER

Tasked with her own mission to hunt down Decepticons, Windblade is a formidable fighter and has the amazing power to create huge wind blasts to destroy her enemies. Her over-confident nature often lands her in trouble but when she joins up with the other Autobots she learns how to plan safer missions and fight as part of a team.

READY FOR ACTION

When the Alchemor crash lands near Denny Clay's scrapyard, his whole life is turned upside down and his home becomes a battle ground. Denny bravely stays to help Team Bee stop the Decepticons reaching Crown City and proves his worth by helping Fixit mend weapons. He's also a mastermind at creating clever plans to keep the Autobots' presence on Earth a secret – a tough job with so many battling bots.

YOUNG ALLY

When Denny's son Russell arrives for a visit, he never expected his dad's scrapyard to be so full of adventure. Smart and brave, Russell quickly shows his loyalty to Team Bee and helps his Autobot friends out with his smart ideas and brave actions.

BUILD A BOT

Customize your own bot! Give them a name, alt mode and add colours, then watch in amazement as Digital Magic brings your unique design to life.

MAKE YOUR OWN TRANSFORMER

Trigger a Transformer to customize yourself, selecting body parts and then colouring them in.

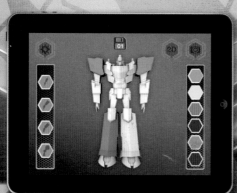